MY WORLD OF SCIENCE

Using Electricity

Revised and Updated

Angela Royston

www.heinemann.co.uk/library
Visit our website to find out more information about Heinemann Library books.

To order:
☎ Phone 44 (0) 1865 888066
🖹 Send a fax to 44 (0) 1865 314091
🖥 Visit the Heinemann Bookshop at www.heinemann.co.uk/library to browse our catalogue and order online.

First published in Great Britain by Heinemann Library, Halley Court, Jordan Hill, Oxford OX2 8EJ, part of Pearson Education. Heinemann is a registered trademark of Pearson Education Ltd.

Editorial: Diyan Leake
Design: Joanna Hinton-Malivoire
Picture research: Melissa Allison and Mica Brancic
Production: Duncan Gilbert

Originated by Chroma Graphics (Overseas) Pte Ltd
Printed and bound in China by South China Printing Co. Ltd

ISBN 978 0 431 13766 7 (hardback)
12 11 10 09 08
10 9 8 7 6 5 4 3 2 1

ISBN 978 0 431 13789 6 (paperback)
12 11 10 09 08
10 9 8 7 6 5 4 3 2 1

British Library Cataloguing in Publication Data
Royston, Angela
  Using electricity. – New ed. – (My world of science)
  1. Electricity – Juvenile literature
  I. Title
  537

Acknowledgements
The publishers would like to thank the following for permission to reproduce photographs: © Corbis pp. 8, 25; © istockphoto.com pp. 5 (Oliver Malms), 7 (Matjaz Boncina and Natalia Bratslavsky); © Pearson Education Ltd/Tudor Photography pp. 12, 14; © Trevor Clifford pp. 6, 9, 10, 11, 13, 15, 16, 17, 18, 19, 20, 21, 22, 23, 24, 26, 27, 28, 29; © Trip p. 4 (H. Rogers).

Cover photograph reproduced with permission of © Masterfile.

The publishers would like to thank Jon Bliss for his assistance in the preparation of this book.

Every effort has been made to contact copyright holders of any material reproduced in this book. Any omissions will be rectified in subsequent printings if notice is given to the publishers.

Contents

Any words appearing in the text in bold, **like this**, are explained in the glossary.

What is electricity?

Electricity is a **power** or **force** that can make something work. For example, electricity makes a bulb light up.

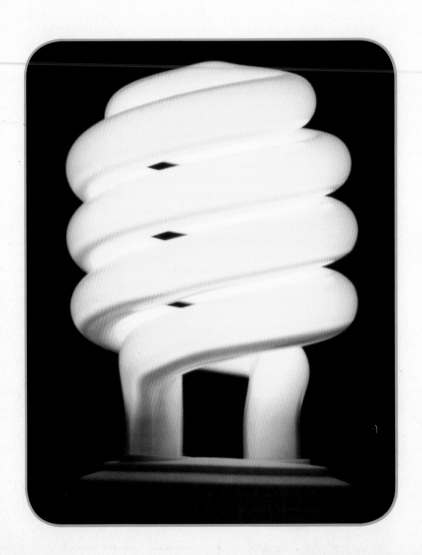

Electricity is used in **machines** in schools, shops, and offices. It is even used in the street. Street lights and signs use electricity to light them.

Using electricity

Electrical **power** can be changed into heat, noise, or movement as well as into light. These **appliances** all use electricity to make heat.

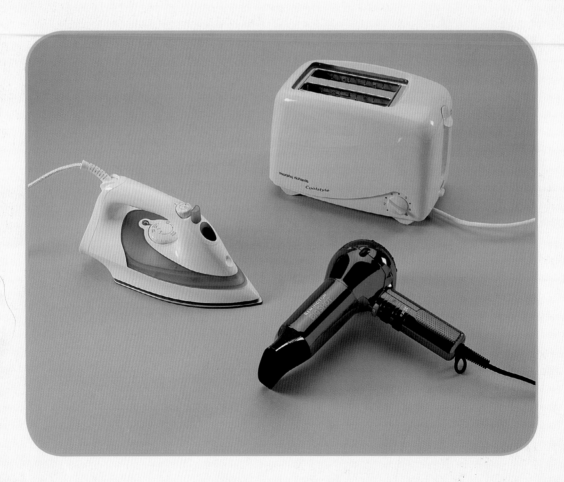

A television uses electricity to make pictures and sounds. A vacuum cleaner uses electricity to suck up dust. It has an electric motor that makes a lot of noise.

Where does electricity come from?

Electricity is made in **power stations**. It is sent along wires to houses, shops, and other buildings. The electrical wires are joined to **sockets** in the wall.

When an electric plug is pushed into a socket, electricity flows into the **machine**. Some sockets have **switches** that stop the electricity flowing.

Danger!

Be careful – electricity is dangerous. An electric shock may hurt or kill you. Never poke things into **sockets** or electrical **machines**.

Once an electric iron, toaster, or oven is hot, it can take a long time to cool down. Be careful not to touch these things after they have been used.

What is a battery?

A battery is a store of electricity. **Chemicals** inside the battery slowly change to make electricity. Batteries are made in different shapes and sizes.

Batteries make only a small amount of electricity and so are very safe. How many batteries does a **remote control** like the one in the picture need to make it work? (Answer on page 31.)

Machines that use batteries

Batteries are useful because you can carry them around. Many small **machines** use batteries so that you can take them around with you.

Batteries do not last for ever. When the batteries in toys are used up, they stop working. You can **recharge** some batteries instead of buying new ones.

Taking a torch apart

Look at one of the batteries inside a torch. One end is flat and has a minus sign (–) on the side. The other end has a bump with a plus sign (+).

Each battery has to be the right way round to make the torch work. The plus end of the battery touches the plus sign in the torch.

What is a circuit?

A **circuit** is a pathway for electricity to flow along. Electricity flows from the battery through the wire, through the light bulb, and back to the battery.

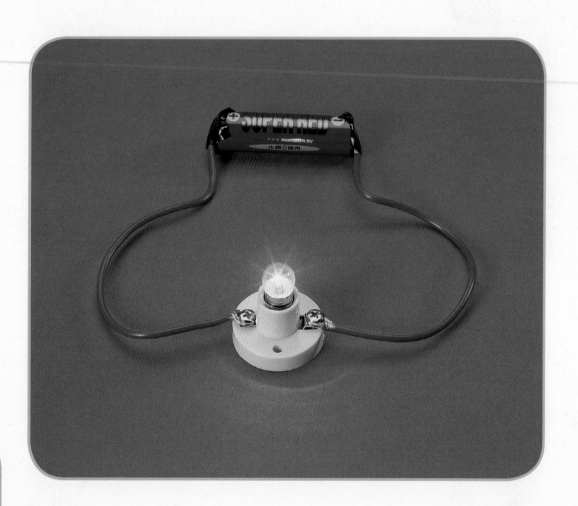

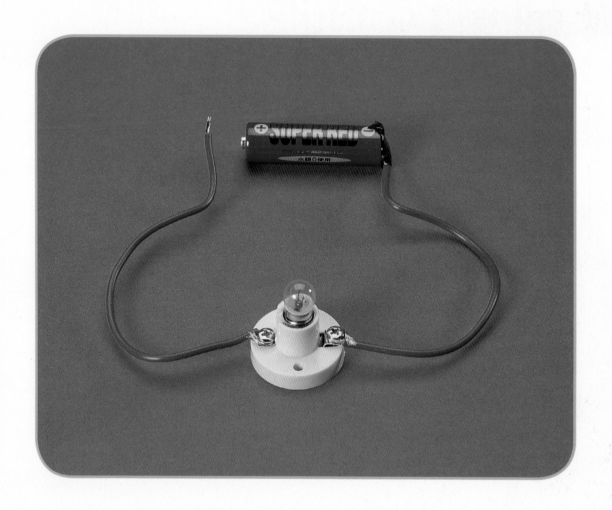

Electricity will flow only if the pathway makes a complete loop. If the loop is broken the electricity stops flowing and the light bulb goes out.

Lighting two bulbs

You can add one or more bulbs to a **circuit**. But every time you add one, the light from each bulb will be dimmer.

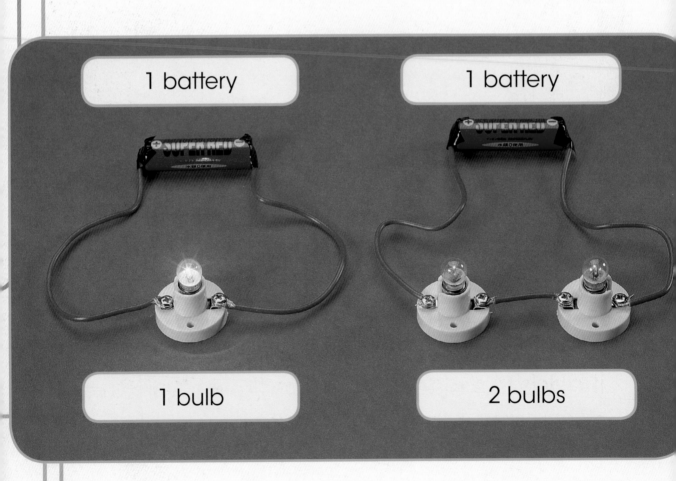

1 battery   1 battery

1 bulb   2 bulbs

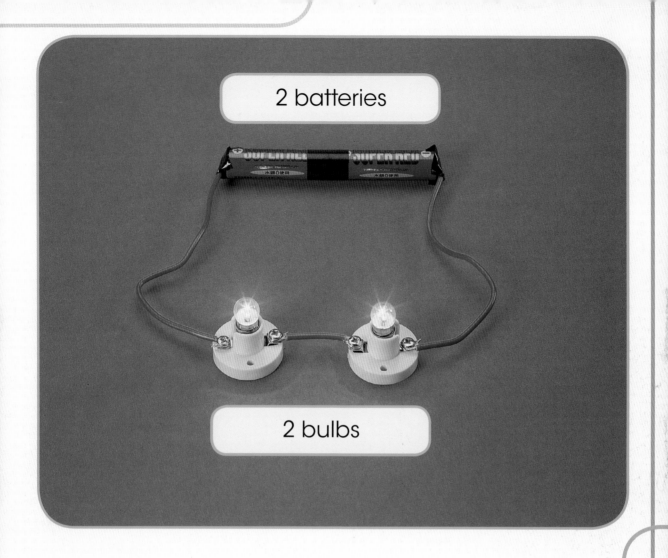

2 batteries

2 bulbs

A battery can only make a fixed amount of electricity. If you add another battery, it adds more electricity. Then the bulbs shine more brightly.

Switches

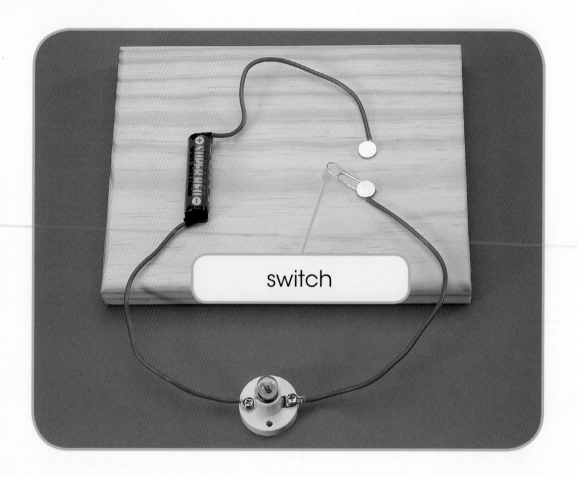

switch

A **switch** is something that can break a **circuit**. When the switch is on, electricity flows around the circuit. When the switch is off, the circuit is broken.

This switch controls an electric train circuit. When the switch is on, the train moves around the track. What happens when the switch is turned off? (Answer on page 31.)

Conductors

A **conductor** is something that lets electricity flow through it easily. This girl is testing metal foil to see how well it conducts electricity.

Metal foil conducts electricity well.
Metal is a good conductor. It is used
for the wires that carry electricity for
electric trains.

Insulators

An **insulator** is something that electricity cannot flow through. Plastic is a good insulator. That is why electrical wires are usually covered with plastic.

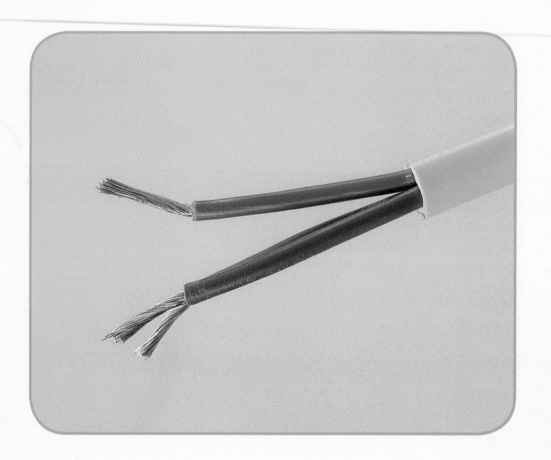

This girl is testing things to see whether they are insulators or conductors. When she tests an insulator, the electricity stops flowing.

Drawing a circuit

You can draw a **circuit** using simple symbols for the battery, **switch**, wire, and bulb. Is the switch in the drawing open or closed? (Answer on page 31.)

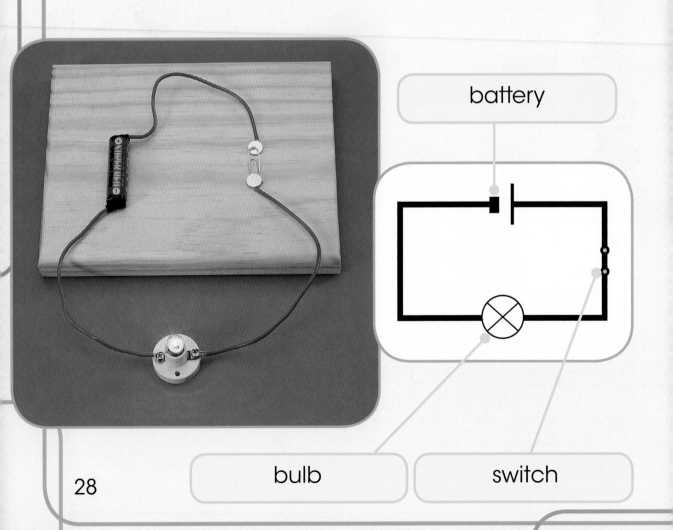

battery

bulb

switch

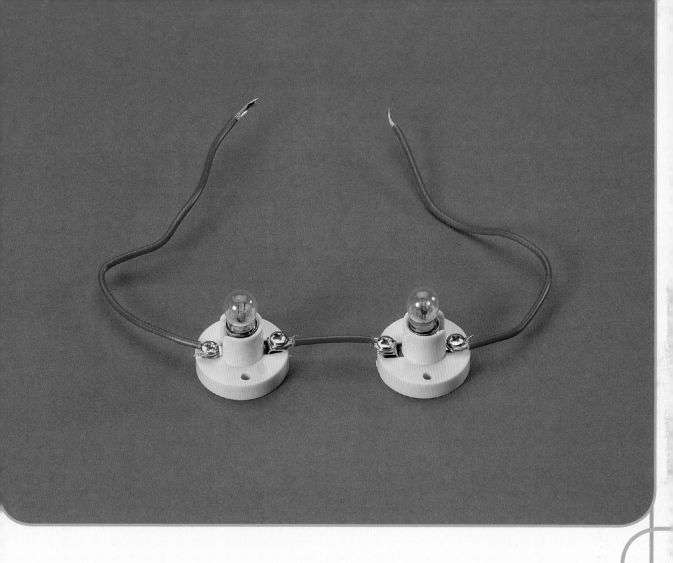

This circuit is not complete. The battery is missing. Make a drawing to show how the circuit should be.

Glossary

appliance equipment that uses electricity in the house

chemical matter that is used to make other matter

circuit pathway that electricity flows along

conductor something that lets electricity flow through it easily

force something that makes things move

insulator something that electricity cannot flow through

machine something that uses force to get something done

power strength or energy

power station building where electricity is made

recharge put more energy in, such as electricity into a battery

remote control something that allows you to turn a machine on and off from a distance

socket hole that an electric plug is fitted into, usually found on the wall

switch something that completes or breaks an electric circuit

Answers

Page 13 – The remote control needs two batteries to make it work.

Page 23 – The train will stop moving when the switch is turned off.

Page 28 – The switch in the circuit is closed.

More books to read

Amazing Science: Electricity, Sally Hewitt (Hodder Wayland, 2006)

Science in Your Life – Electricity: Turn it on! Wendy Sadler (Raintree, 2005)

Start-up Science: Electricity, Claire Llewellyn (Evans, 2004)

Index